Vintage and Artistic Homes *of Boulder*

AUTHOR & PHOTOGRAPHER

GAYL GRAY

JOHNSON BOOKS
BOULDER

gaylie@comcast.net

ISBN: 978-1-55566-447-3

For more information about fine books from Johnson Books, a Big earth Publishing company, please contact your local bookstore, call us at 1-800-258-5830, or visit us on the web at bigearthpublishing.com

Johnson Books
a Big Earth Publishing company
3360 Mitchell Lane, Suite E
Boulder, Colorado 80301

Printed in China

CONTENTS

Preface

As a photographer I'm very attracted to architecture, lured by the flourish of a façade. For me, an interior full of memories or the expression of artistic preference in a room can be irresistible. Here, my focus is a variety of eras and styles of homes in my town.

As the owners speak to me, they explain their experience with their dwellings; Boulder's historic personality and design development emerge. Owners' decorating solutions appear, too. In a city of unlimited creativity, there's so much to discover.

MAPLETON
ALL

Mapleton Elementary School, 1888

Mapleton Hill

Cabin in the City

A cabin on Mapleton Hill? That was natural in 1923. Then, this house, surrounded by and partially constructed of country fieldstones, was on an undeveloped street. Two buildings nearby housed farm animals.

The fieldstones were still in place when the owners, two former teachers of French and Spanish, acquired it in 1967. The house, however, had been expanded and the outbuildings no longer existed. At that time, the dense shade of a buckeye chestnut, the Ohio state tree, appeared as it does today. It's about seventy years old, and is a rare variety here.

The teachers love to build, decorate, and landscape, and the former cabin's park-sized backyard gives them room to pursue these interests. A few years ago, they took on their own kitchen remodel to create a European farmstead ambience. They explored faux-finish methods, learning how to apply a glaze layer to a couple of different colors underneath,

achieving a marbleized effect. They couldn't decide on a favorite tile, so they acquired many Mediterranean varieties to combine in the room.

The backyard is so alluring that the owners extended their living and dining areas to meet it. They bumped out walls, added lots of glass, and enlarged the flagstone floor.

For ages they'd wanted to connect the patio and the upstairs deck with a wrought-iron stairway. Traveling in the south, they'd seen examples, climbing with flowers, especially on the Battery in Charleston, South Carolina. New staircases were so expensive that after years of searching, they visited the Resource Yard, a Boulder home-materials recycle center. To their amazement, they found their metal steps, with just a couple of inches to trim before installation.

Over the years they have terraced their park, which consists of two levels. The meadow at the west end of the land has stately trees and a creek, the very

items the owners were seeking when they moved in.

The terracing evolved sequentially as the couple planned to host wedding receptions for family and friends. Recently they held a birthday celebration in the meadow with a bluegrass band and a caller for square dancing.

Harmonizing with an Antique

Growing up in the American suburbs of the 1970s, this couple ever after preferred vintage living quarters. Moving to an 1877 Italianate townhouse fulfilled their major requirements: "authentically old and near the city." They like to walk to restaurants, bookstores, and coffee shops. "It's sociable—we get a chance to see neighbors," they say. The two share an enthusiasm for cooking and enjoy a convivial existence, including the summer hosting of visiting Colorado Music Festival instrumentalists.

This Mapleton Hill home accommodates their lifestyle, and they have the skills to nourish the historic landmark. E.H. Dimick, architect of Old Main on the CU campus, also created their home, the Earhart-Degge House.

The spouses have distinct specialties in home renovation. She researches and applies the paint (deep rose, yellow curry). With software from Benjamin Moore, she tests a variety of colors using online photos of the rooms. To bring out the

decorative white moldings and ceiling rosettes, she painted overhead surfaces the same color as the walls.

What's left? Almost everything in terms of building and maintenance can be done by her husband, or, in his words, "Whatever the house needs." He enjoys carpentry, so he built a cork floor and bookshelf for the library. He also plans and installs house lighting.

They choose and hang art before deciding on wall colors. Their collection includes two Thai temple doors

and a French railroad station clock. They choose paintings both locally and during travels.

The house is named for its principal historic inhabitants. Dr. William R. Earhart had a medical practice in and around Boulder during the late 1800s. His former office is now the home's kitchen.

William W. Degge was a real estate developer and owner of significant Boulder acreage. He and his family lived in this house over the first seven decades of the twentieth century. The current owners met some of the Degge descendents when the house was part of a Historic Boulder tour in 2003.

401

The Lewis-Cobb House

Edwin C. Lewis commissioned William Lee Woollett to design this house, which was built in 1904. In 1944, gold miner Harrison Cobb purchased the house and stayed for several decades.

William Lee Woollett was an architect from Albany, New York. A couple of years after the 1906 San Francisco earthquake, he moved to California where he designed art deco theatres in Los Angeles, along with many other buildings.

With its horizontal lines, this house's style has a Prairie appearance. Prairie is a design originated by Frank Lloyd Wright and popular in the first two decades of the twentieth century.

The home's current owners are the Holum family, who came to Mapleton Hill from San Francisco. There, they could walk to town. In Boulder, they can do that and also be located close to the mountains.

An outstanding feature of this house is the porch, where one can practically live. There are dining and relaxing spaces. From the porch one can converse with passing neighbors. This veranda has views to the red rocks, and its fir floor could host a waltz with a string quartet.

The brick walls are eighteen inches thick, and, unexpectedly, the house includes a five-hundred-square-foot bomb shelter. The hand-chipped exterior brick requires more than the usual processing and application. It is Flemish bond; the bond, or pattern, has both short and long horizontal shapes, placed so they alternate in the overall pattern. The short bricks are glazed a contrasting black.

The tile on the living room fireplace is called Moravian and was originated by Henry Mercer, a participant in the Arts and Crafts movement in early twentieth-century Bucks County, Pennsylvania. The tile's name comes from the Moravian Church in Pennsylvania where Mercer copied his earliest designs.

The Holums wanted to add more light to the upstairs area and also to modernize it. At the same time, they would continue living with the quiet, efficient radiators and the perfect fir floors.

The upstairs interior design experience was in-depth and felt creative, assisted by a designer friend's guidance. Wall colors were lightened. The bath became what homeowners choose today—separate shower and tub, and two sinks. New light fixtures from the Denver Design Center and the West End Gardener added art to the mix.

A Norwegian friend and artist contributed a large mountain canvas, and he also drew the rosemaling design now carved on some of the cabinet doors. Rosemaling is a traditional Norwegian folk art that uses scrollwork and geometric elements.

When the Holums first arrived, they found a house that was well maintained. It's always been a kind of city attraction, and the family hosts community events there. They have enjoyed calling it home over the last twenty years.

401

Maplehurst

Like other families, the Brunels have lived in more than one home within Boulder's historic district. They relocated from a Maxwell Street house to an 1890 shingle Victorian built by Fred Lockwood, owner of several mercantile businesses in the Boulder area.

The shingle Victorian is a style originating in the seaside regions of the northeastern United States. It is characterized by an irregularly shaped structure that is unified by the smooth outer surface of the upper-story shingles. This type of Victorian was primarily designed by high-fashion architects and built between 1880 and 1900.

In 2000, 110 years after Maplehurst was built, the Brunels moved in, having renovated the Victorian's interior. Their project aimed for contemporary taste while respecting the home's original era.

One element they favored was wainscot, a paneling style usually applied to the lower part of an interior wall. In the family room, the ceiling is coffered and finished with sunken panels in the shape of a square. Generous wood detailing adds intimacy to large rooms.

The family brought along a few well-loved decorations from their former historic home to this one: two light fixtures and the banister's newel-post top.

Several decorative items, like two Venetian sconces, came from one source: the owner's aunt's collection at a Denver antique store on Broadway.

On the exterior, a large variety of finishing materials and shapes draw the eye and work well together—the rafter tails are an example. Also, there are three shapes of shingles: diamond, scallop, and square. When designing their addition to Maplehurst, the Brunels chose other and fewer shingle patterns to meet National Historic guidelines: Anything added on to the structure should have a distinct appearance to show it's not original.

The house has a couple of Romeo-and-Juliet (small-sized) balconies on the second floor. One is original; the second one the couple replicated on a larger scale for outside their bedroom.

David Brunel is an entrepreneur currently investigating biotechnology. His wife, Stacey Steers, is an artistic animator whose film was featured at the Denver Art Museum in 2011. Brunel is a vegetable gardener and likes fruit trees, while Steers focuses on the mostly perennial flowerbeds.

The silver maples, planted in the late 1800s in this neighborhood and succumbing to old age, continue to provide plenty of shade. Two flowers chosen for Maplehurst's landscape supply lengthy blooming seasons at the front of the property and elsewhere: a white autumn anemone and a coral Meidiland rose.

Painting the Trim Peach

(As told by Steve McIntosh)

This Carpenter Gothic style of Victorian house was built in 1879 as part of the Squires Addition, one of the earliest real estate developments in Boulder. It was characterized by walls of lath and plaster, without insulation, and piped for gas lighting. When I acquired it in 1990, one of the things I did was to ask Alameda Ornamental Iron to design an authentic Victorian-style wrought-iron fence. My wife Tehya and I developed a couple of rooms that recreate Victorian times. Working with Bradbury and Bradbury, a dealer in period wallpapers and fabrics, we upgraded the paint scheme to be high Victorian, as can be seen in the Neo-Greek trim on our dining room walls.

Victorian structures have architectural features that appeal to me. There's the ornate decoration, like the floral motif on our front gable. Such trim was available and frequently duplicated because the Industrial Revolution allowed mass production of what had been a fine craft. These houses also feature substantial dining rooms that promote family togetherness and entertaining, wraparound porches that center the outdoor activity in connection with the community, and dramatic, high ceilings.

Before living here, I bought a redwood Victorian in the Western Addition of San Francisco near Haight-Ashbury. There, the richly exuberant style had been attracting hippies for some time; their psychedelic sensibility contributed significantly to the "painted lady" look of those houses. In the 1950s, Victorian abodes were considered ugly, and for a period after that time, could be purchased cheaply.

I never thought that I would live in a historic house, but I fell so in love with the one I had in San Francisco that I became a connoisseur of Victorian style. Included in my reading were the books *Painted Ladies* and *Painted Ladies Revisited;* these depict San Francisco's Victorian homes. The original paint colors featured earth tones, umbers, and dark reds. For our Boulder place, when we recently needed to make repairs, we wanted a bright and cheery color combination, hence the peach, butter-cream, and sage green that now decorate the house.

Renovating Like it's 1892

The present residents of this handsome mansion on Mapleton Hill added a room and renewed the paint and decorative touches throughout. After more than a century of varying ownership, many features of Dodge House's original appearance would be restored.

The house had been built in the early 1890s by Horace O. Dodge, a former Civil War physician whose regiment opened the Battle of Gettysburg. In Boulder, Dodge helped create a hospital, served as county physician and coroner, and taught at CU, among many energetic contributions.

Beginning in 1989, as the current occupants restored their new home, it would display the same overhead surfaces in the added family room as it had in its original spaces. The ceilings are coved—a curve joins the wall and ceiling, eliminating sharp corners.

Walls are made of the lath (wood strip) and plaster used during that era. When the residents repainted, they found three layers of wallpaper. They also discovered horsehair mixed with the plaster—for reinforcement.

Lath and plaster was easily shattered when nineteenth-century householders tried to put nails in the walls to hang pictures. That's why picture molding was incorporated into room design in those days. Now,

Dodge House's owners have installed the molding to maintain the style that would likely have been featured in such a home.

Rope-and-pulley operation continues to exist in several of the home's windows. From 1850 to 1945, window technology consisted of two cast-iron weights totaling the exact weight of a window sash, making it hang perfectly. Today's windows function with spring-loaded systems. The owners found a rope-and-pulley specialist to maintain the original tradition of their century-old windows.

Painting trim a variety of colors is today's innovation. This home features exterior dentils—a series of closely spaced rectangular blocks that form a molding. To emphasize their appearance,

each small square has had its face painted a subtle deep green, using a small brush.

The prominent cupola on the roof was missing its original decoration. The owners employed a self-taught fine-carpentry craftsman and early architecture scholar. "When Horace Dodge's great-granddaughter gave us early photos taken here, we were amazed at how closely our friend and woodworker had been able to restore what had disappeared from the cupola's design," they relate.

Throughout Dodge House, replicas of elegant original carvings and furniture created for the owners by this woodworking artist appear. "If we need to know the height of an 1890s kitchen baseboard [12 inches], he's our go-to guy," note the residents.

Whittier

Queen Anne Gets Dressed Up

This 1883 Queen Anne Victorian was built by William R. Whitmore, a speculator in Leadville's mines. Current owners Larry and Bonnie Gossman found a miner's pick while terracing their backyard.

The Whitmore family, with community connections such as the Boulder Philharmonic Club and the CU Electrical Engineering Department, remained here until 1919.

The house was part of the fill-in for a block containing several grand dwellings. The neighborhood developed to reflect the character of its professional and middle-class inhabitants—the homes possess a variety of styles ranging from craftsman to Italianate.

Then and now, this Whittier neighborhood block has contained homes and businesses. Larry Gossman owns American Village Restoration. He creates, refinishes, restores, and replicates works in wood, assisted by Bonnie. He is able to repair a Victorian chair or build a new reredos (ornamental partition behind an altar), as he did for St. John's Episcopal Church nearby. Larry can also faux finish a dresser top to make it look like marble.

The couple created their Victorian's fretwork (ornate woodwork of interlacing designs) after purchasing the home in 1970. The house is finished with straight-sided, round-bottomed "fish-scale" shingles that were used extensively on Victorians. It lacked much of the traditional gingerbread found on more opulent homes.

The Gossmans fashioned both atypical (wrought iron) and characteristic trim. The wooden filigree includes the acanthus leaf design. A characteristic Victorian icon, it originated with the Greeks and Romans because it grew where they quarried the marble they used for building.

After thoughtfully embellishing the house's exterior and interior spaces, the Gossmans commented, "Our hope is to add to the history of this house while we're here, and leave it better than we found it when we're gone."

Impulse Buy

(As told by Alice Norton)

I grew up in Alton, Illinois, where there were nice examples of Italianate houses—even one in our family. I love old homes and architecture, and when West Pearl became a historic district, I worked on the guidelines as a member of Historic Boulder.

In 2005, while living in an older home at Fifth and Pearl, I attended an open house in the Whittier neighborhood for the sleekly Italianate Austin House. The attraction was so complete I decided to buy it on the spot. Eugene Austin had it built in 1875. He ran a brick-making operation that served the university campus. He was also one of Boulder's mayors.

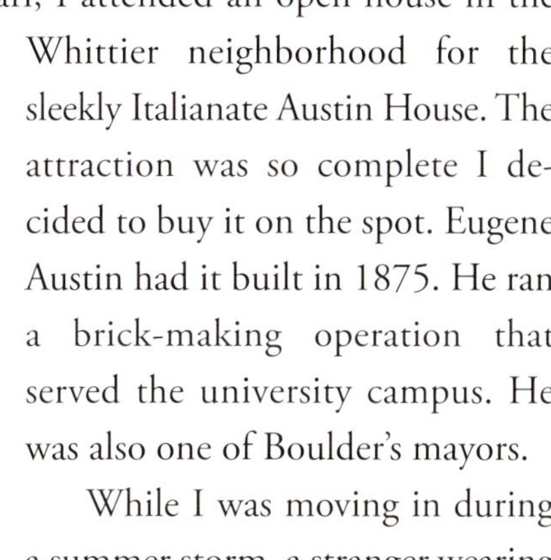

While I was moving in during a summer storm, a stranger wearing a raincoat was photographing my new home. He turned out to be Austin's great-great grandson, who was in town for a brief visit. I talked with him, and through that chance encounter, I now possess historic pictures of the house and its original owner.

I am the Executive Director of the AMC Cancer Fund, and at Christmas, friends and colleagues enjoy gathering in my dining room with its cherry red walls. The floors, which are now so thin they cannot be refinished, are decorated with a contrasting Greek key inlay. In this room and others, the steel ceilings are of the type made by Mesker and Company.

In 1846, German immigrant John Mesker started a tinning and ironworks company. Eventually his sons joined the business,

and the company continues to exist today. At the turn of the nineteenth century, its pressed metal ceilings were sold in catalogs and easily shipped to customers by rail.

The Whittier neighborhood is great for a stroll past the architectural wonders of its many churches and diversely styled historic houses. There's an active neighborhood group for shared get-togethers, and I'm within walking distance of many of Boulder's fine restaurants, BMoCA, and the farmer's market.

Eben G. Fine Park

West Arapahoe

Destined to Decorate

(As told by Sid and Kathy Freudenstein)

When I bought this house in 1975, it seemed that the former owners preferred a 1950s look to the Victorian style. They hadn't destroyed, but had hidden many of this 1902 Queen Anne's decorations with Formica and plywood. The original fancy trim wasn't noticeable on a house that was predominantly painted mint-ice-cream green," says scientist Sidney Freudenstein.

"Over the years I've lived here, and when [wife] Kathy joined me, we've needed to expand the house, and have accentuated its original style. The façade's shape has not changed, though a widow's walk [railed rooftop platform] disappeared before my ownership.

"Prior to moving in, I had a couple of weeks to shore up the crumbling walls of the interior. I wanted to make them look as they originally had, so I consulted some of the founders of Historic Boulder. They visited me in this neighborhood, Highland Lawn, and showed me how to plaster walls in the traditional way.

"A growing family, including six grandkids and our lifestyle, dictated additions; we expanded this 850-square-foot home to 2,400 as needs came up. Our friend and architect, Charles Deane, created the designs for the spaces we added. These include the upstairs, living room, dining room, the loggia [arcade with open sides] and patios."

Kathy recalls, "My dad was a Miami architect, so our family always received art supplies for Christmas. Dad would take us to his building sites, and we did simple home projects like painting and furniture refinishing.

"When I wanted a new dining area for this house, I discovered encaustic tile. A pattern is inlaid into the body of the tile, so that as the tile is worn down, the design remains," she says.

"These tiles were most often used in churches during the medieval era and up to the nineteenth century. There are two

sisters in Miami who travel Europe and collect them from demolition projects.

"The tiles we got from that company had been part of an ancient church in France. Sid and I installed them. They were a bear to work with because every tile needed an energetic cleaning. The tiles' shapes were irregular, too, but we got the job done. Charles Deane says it's one of his favorite floors.

"I also installed the Venetian plaster in the dining room. You apply and burnish it three times. Sid made the bookshelves here in the living room. We found the design on a trip to England."

Sid adds, "My mother bought me carpentry tools and when I was fourteen, my first project was a screened-in porch for our house. I've since figured out how to do the electrical and plumbing work needed here. As the house has expanded, I've learned to

add interior and exterior trim that appears as it would have in 1902. For example, I matched the thickness of the new flagstone sills to that of the original ones."

Kathy comments on the couple's art collection: "I wanted art in the house, so I started painting. A lot of what you see here comes from that hobby of mine. I like to do scenes from our travels to Venice and elsewhere.

"We also like to garden, and the 'Victorian cottage' look does get noticed. The house once appeared on a Denver Water Board poster used for promoting Xeriscape."

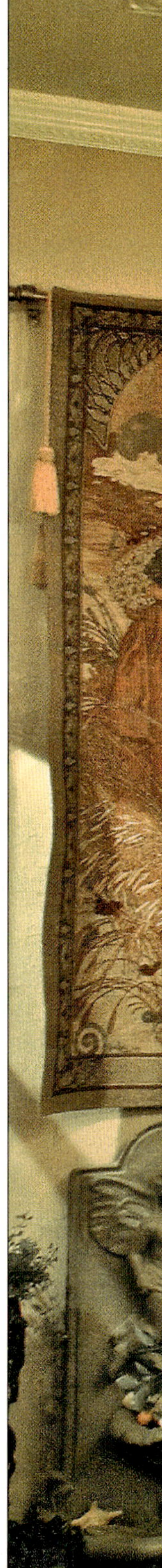

A Different Kind of Puzzle

(As told by Ed Phelps)

I'm a software developer with two kids age twelve and fourteen. Fifteen years ago I moved to Boulder from Virginia, and six years ago I purchased my [French] Second Empire Victorian house. This style has arches over the windows, decorative brackets and a mansard roof. The mansard was popular because its shape allowed for the building of a full upper story within the roof's attic space.

In the 1880s, Millard F. Leech lived in the house, which had been built at the beginning of the decade. The house was about the only thing on this block of the West Arapahoe neighborhood. Leech was a mining engineer for the Switzerland Trail, a railroad that provided transit from Boulder to mountain locations like Gold Hill and Ward. In the 1950s, the house sold for $12,500, and it became a boarding establishment. In the 1960s it served as a preschool. For me, it's close to town and the bike path—fabulous for raising kids.

In repairing and updating the house, my goal was to replicate the original scale and materials. It's like working a puzzle to do that; as part of the process you've got to combine a modern lifestyle with a former era. We scaled the property's first garage to the dimensions of the house. We needed a deeper porch, and we incorporated the old porch materials, or had posts turned to match.

Sometimes we just couldn't use the original materials. For example, we needed a new roof. I decided on tin as a material that wouldn't compete with other aspects of the original design, but would conform with current laws.

I like the colors purple and green, so I included them in updating interior spaces like the kitchen. For exterior painting, we chose those colors as a base and then added the lavender, yellow, and cream. My goal was to accentuate the trim. Choosing colors took forever; we went through dozens.

I collect local art that I find at shows like Open Studios and the Cherry Creek Arts Festival because I like getting to know the artists from whom I buy. What I have includes sculpture by Cha Cha, and a couple of paintings by Jake Johanson. His painting, part of the photo of my dining room, and many more of his originals, now appear on skateboard decks.

Growing a Sculpture Garden

(As told by Kevan Krasnoff)

Twenty-seven years ago, I needed an art studio. On the grounds of a hundred-year-old farm and orchard I found one in Boulder's West Arapahoe neighborhood. Later the property came up for sale, and after figuring out how to buy it, I began clearing the property.

This touched off a major process that involved what I did for a living and what was on the land I'd just acquired. It was full of old steel and leftover crazy stuff and I noticed: I'm removing scrap steel, yet I'm bringing in steel materials so I can make sculpture.

I was also doing landscaping and stonework assignments at that time, and would end up with bits and pieces of materials left over from those jobs. As I arranged my property, there was an organic development where I grouped added objects, balancing their relationship with each other. Nature would then take over and give the staging harmony with plants and vines.

It was a chaotic approach to what became the sculpture garden, seen by visitors to events like Open Studios, or by appointment year round. In January, the starkness of the space is very energetic.

The garden's development is continuous. I do paintings, ceramics, and works in steel. My Boulder friends and I share our art. When a piece is sold or exchanged for something else, the one highly considered aspect is finding the appropriate place to install it.

Lotus House

Frances Higgins, a producer at the city of Boulder's Channel 8, walks through her colorfully art-filled home, and after a compliment on the art, she says, "Oh, thanks, a friend painted that," and "I took an art class and did those."

Seated in the "first" parlor, she comments, "I love the parlor and the pocket doors. In olden times, a new beau was only allowed to meet in the first parlor with his lady." These days, getting ready for an occasional siesta, Higgins first closes the massive and original caramel-colored doors on both sides of the parlor.

"We only needed to renovate the kitchen and baths, and then we found, under the wallpaper, an old postcard from a young man to a young woman living in the house. He wrote that he'd come by on horseback, but was disappointed not to have found her at home," she says.

This sturdy, intact dwelling in Highland Lawn, an independent community until 1891, was built in 1895. Its style is Edwardian Vernacular, utilizing the forms of the Victorian age, but dispensing with frilly decoration and employing more classical details. In this case, the ogee arch graces various elements of the façade. It is a double-curve shape introduced from the Arab world in the fourteenth century. It became popular throughout medieval England, and was also a favorite in ancient Venice.

The small decorative panes in the upper part of the façade's main window echo the ogee-arch shape. Small panes encased many windows until the mid-nineteenth century, when panes came to be glazed in increasing size. This particular glass was not a technological necessity.

When the former owner of this house wanted to give it historic designation, he named it Lotus House. A lotus today is a water lily; in Greek mythology it was the fruit of a shrub, which when eaten, brought forgetfulness. This house, however, was named after the owner's Lotus sports car, an exotic vehicle manufactured over the past fifty years.

"We [Higgins and her husband Elliott, a dentist] moved here from Sugarloaf when the kids got to be school age. We wanted them to be able to walk to school. We knew this neighborhood as a friendly one. Our kids grew up playing at the creek on the rope swings. When the water ran high and fast, they'd ride waves with their boogie boards."

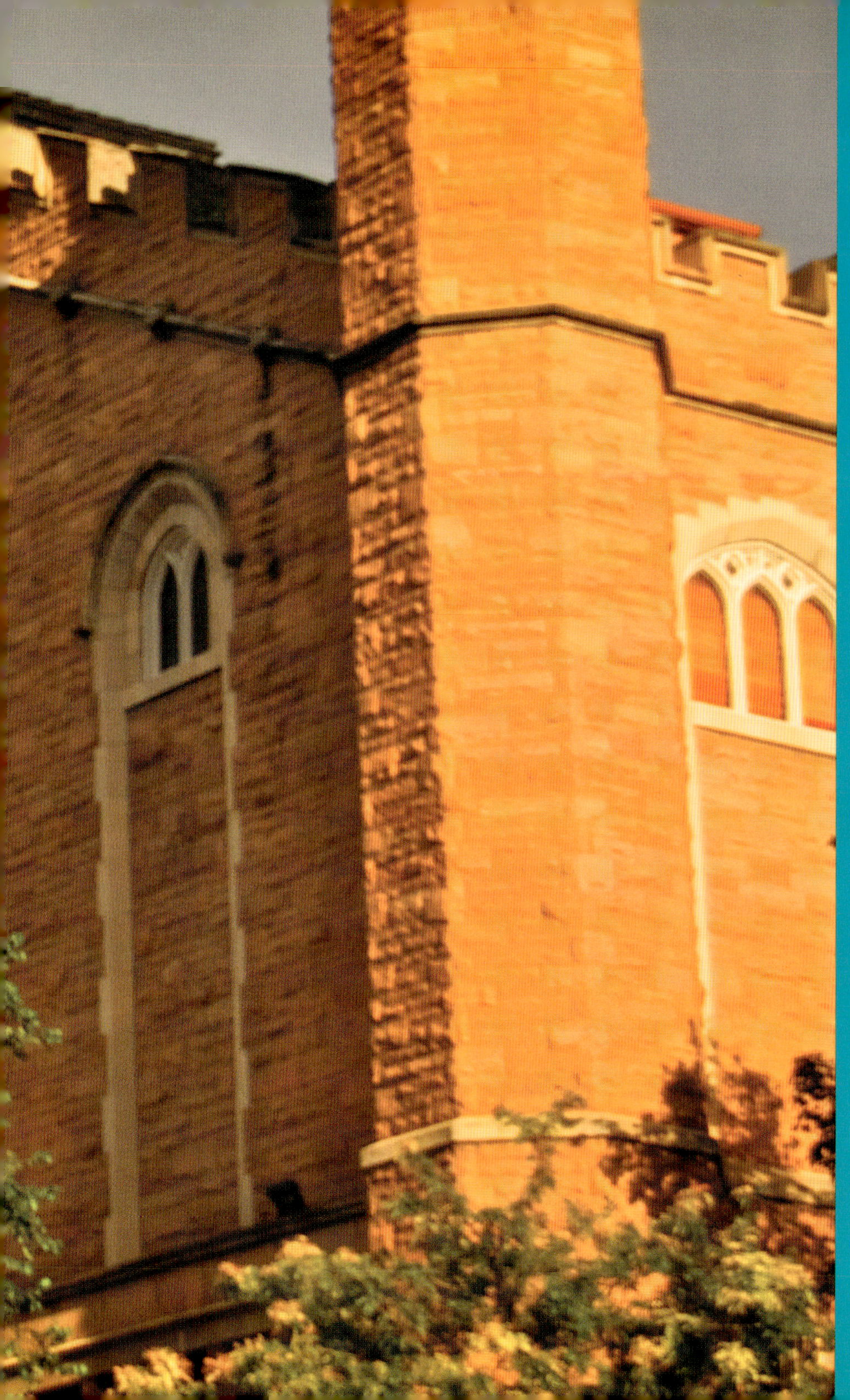

University Hill

Macky Auditorium, opened in 1923 on the University of Colorado campus

Rose Hill Cottage

In the midst of Chautauqua Heights sits the periodically transformed Rose Hill Cottage. The Rea family, who once lived across the street, built the cottage for their daughter in 1898. The Reas owned extensive property near Chautauqua, and, for decades, had grown vegetables, owned several homes, and supplied the mines in Boulder. The foundation of Rose Hill Cottage is stone from Woods Quarry, now a part of Boulder's Mesa Trail.

A century after the appearance of the cottage, the present owners were drawn to it through their interest in classic homes and eclectic neighborhoods. Some original architecture remained: the arched

windows and the front door with its Victorian design, for example. The new owners wanted to honor the home's original concept.

They obtained photos of it from1899, which showed the house with an unobstructed view to the Flatirons. The photos revealed a long-absent wraparound porch as the original front of the cottage. The modern buyers recreated that porch, and stripped "what must have been eighty layers" off the front door to find its lacy valentine carving. Wood carving that appears to have been created by the same local artist is visible on the Rea House across the street.

700

Needing additional space at Rose Hill Cottage, the current owners decided to decorate their planned upper story with a hexagonal dormer, echoing the half-hexagon shapes of the original windows. They added that type of dormer to a new wing, as well. The addition includes recessed arched windows with carved stone sills to match those installed in the original structure.

Today, along the stairway that connects the two stories, is a modern metal banister with a Victorian design by Metal Magic in Louisville.

Another standout addition to the interior is the chocolate-cream granite kitchen countertops from Brazil. Once the kitchen was complete, tarts made their appearance from the oven. Their red apples came from the one tree left at the cottage from Rose Hill's former orchards.

561

The Art and Craft of a Victorian

Tina Collen, a graphic designer and artist in many genres, arrived in Boulder in 1992, to help her son Mark remodel his house. "I decided to live in Boulder at that time; then, a for-sale sign appeared across the street from Mark's place. I bought the house immediately—a psychic had predicted that I'd live across the street from my son," she says.

Collen does follow her instincts, as when, after the purchase of the 1889 Victorian-era cottage, she undertook a year of piano lessons. "A music teacher spent most of her long life here. I kept getting professional mail for her; finally I felt the urge to learn how to play a piece. I took lessons, and now can perform Claire de Lune." She laughs.

After purchasing the house, she lived on the property while it was being remodeled. The walls, the brick façade, and a mullioned window are original. "Living on-site let me see deeply into the way things were developing, with the result that I live in a space that suits me perfectly," says the owner.

Collen became the general contractor on her west Boulder renovation. "I sensed a resistance to following the instructions of a woman, especially one with unusual ideas," she says in answer to a query about the experience.

For example, she wanted the oak floor laid diagonally; her contractor was unfamiliar with the concept. Her insistence resulted in a living space that flows smoothly from one area to the next.

"It's unusual for me to get angry, but I considered acting lessons during that management experience. At the 'wrap party,' though, the contractors agreed it was worth it," she says.

While it's obviously a dwelling, there's enough art here to fill a gallery. One room is so-named and is outfitted with appropriate seating and lighting. Collen has done many types of visual art, but her highest-profile work is the "Fleurotica" collages displayed in this cozy gallery space.

Her most recent idea was several years in the making. It's an "artobiography," detailing her life and art, which was published in 2010 as *Storm of the i.*

House of Many Colors

As a young man, Albert Alhadeff left New York for Boulder to teach art history at the University of Colorado. Early on, his desire for a one-of-a-kind home led to a perfect working relationship with Boulder architect Rigomar Thurmer, a student of Philip Johnson and Mies van der Rohe.

"I asked Rigo to design a Boullee for me," says Alhadeff. (Centuries ago, architect Etienne-Louis Boullee had proposed a structure in the shape of a sphere.) Thurmer replied, "I can't do a Boullee; what would you think about a Van Doesburg?" This was a reference to a twentieth-century artist and architect heavily influenced by Mondrian.

Alhadeff liked the idea. He also couldn't help recognizing that the proposed design in planes and rectangles would cost less to build than his original notion.

He had purchased land near Chautauqua Park in the early '70s. By 1979, with Thurmer's design, he had the house he wanted. "I loved those extended planes, and the long walls and right angles made me happy. I appreciate original architecture and I was living in it," he comments.

In the coming years, Albert wanted to add a studio, then a bedroom and bath upstairs. In cooperation with friends, his wife, Cha You Jeong, and architects, he remodeled in a way he considers consistent with the home's original design.

At the Museum of Modern Art he'd seen an exhibit featuring the work of Luis Barragan, Mexico's most distinguished twentieth-century architect. Barragan's creations feature vast planes of pinks, oranges, ochres, and blues. "I was focused on his color combinations and found the colors I was looking for at Home Depot in the Ralph Lauren line of paints," Alhadeff relates.

"I wanted deeply saturated exterior surfaces. I found it was possible to have stucco wall material mixed with my paint choices." The result is walls with permanent color.

Contemporary Craftsman

(As told by Sonja Tuitele)

Between the two of us, we'd looked at 150 houses by the time we found this one in 2008. As we desired, it was recently remodeled and had views of the Flatirons. There are two master suites—great for our parents, who like to visit.

The open, connected floor plan lets us entertain guests at the kitchen island, while the kids play a couple of steps down in the family room.

My husband Ken sells software and is also part owner of a gym. I'm a marketer for the natural foods industry. A big focus for us is music—both listening and playing. Dancing is another family household pastime.

We love the front perennial garden that keeps on blooming from spring through fall. Longtime gardener for this house, Chris Smith, is passionate to see it continue to do well.

The architectural style is contemporary (1993) craftsman. Though we're centrally located on Seventh and Aurora, in winter, the snow piles up around the house, making us feel we're in the mountains.

The house originally was designed both for privacy and to take advantage of the light and scenery. In the bedrooms upstairs, we have wonderful mountain views. On the north side, quite close to the next property, there are just two glass-block windows.

My dad lives in Hawaii and is able to trade his accounting work to an artist, Luigi Fumagali. His work is part of what gives our interior its vibe. The decorative ceiling fans and light fixtures are from Splashlight.

Seventh Street is historically quite interesting. There's the former home of Scott Carpenter. He named his spacecraft Aurora Seven, but apparently only realized the sentimental coincidence later.

Also on this block are stone residences where multiple generations have lived; summer visitors built homes resembling the Chautauqua cabins here, too.

At four a.m. last summer, seeing bears with the help of a flashlight was a treat. They forage in the alley, though we've locked our garbage cans and haven't a thing to offer them.

Building Back in Time

Doug and Joan Raymond had lived in Boulder a decade ago, and they missed it. In 2008, they found a property in Geneva Park, at the base of the Flatirons. Their architect suggested a style reminiscent of an Italian farmhouse. As frequent visitors to Italy, the couple found the idea intriguing.

Inspiration came from architect Sam Austin's take on home design. He wanted to use recycled building materials that he was discovering at Denver's Mendoza Used Brick. Joan says that this trove of antiques generated an abundance of ideas for the architect, the builders, and the owners.

Austin selected formerly used column capitals, keystones, crown molding (fancy upper trim), stone, and brick. He then transformed a capital into a bench support and placed the keystone upside-down on its arch.

Granite in the house comes from an assortment of leftover scraps; each room with a countertop displays a unique granite color and design. Joan comments, "It's fun not to have things matchy-matchy."

There's a concentration on natural materials. The landscape architect for the project, Thomas Altgelt, traveled to Wyoming to obtain hefty boulders for specific locations, and he used several to create water features. A principle for this project dictated that the landscaping develop simultaneously with the progress of the building.

The wine storage room has a ceiling constructed of groined vaults. Their geometric form creates strength without massive buttress formations; they were first used by the Romans.

From the streets in ancient Rome, houses were nondescript. "When you were invited in, that's where the nice things were," says Joan. Hidden throughout this property are special features waiting to be discovered.

1
5
2
9

Now You See It

While taking a walk in the Chautauqua neighborhood, a dose of personality focused me on the property to my left for the first time. Why had I never been drawn to this Spanish Revival dwelling and magical surrounding property? Actually, it had just materialized—built by its owner Geoffrey Simpson from the ground up in 2007, using all recycled materials. The land had formerly been occupied by an asbestos ranch house.

Meticulously sought-out architectural materials give this dwelling its timeless quality. Its architecture gives it nostalgia. The arched doorway and stucco exterior denote Spanish Revival style. The low-pitched red roof is mission style with its half-cylinder shaped tiles. Decorative iron sconces and an iron-railed balcony are central to Spanish colonial tradition. Gardens of roses and hospitable touches surrounding the property complete this unexpected homage to the Alhambra.

The Andrew/Hauck House

This is a distinctive dwelling, yet due to its overall color and placement on the property, it could easily escape notice. It's a rare example in Boulder—a substantial, historic, Spanish Revival house. Situated on a hill, it features stucco, tile, wrought iron, and an arcaded porch with semicircular arches. The architectural trim and the color accents form a well-conceived counterpoint to the stately design.

Originally it was a handsome, sturdy Edwardian Vernacular home built around 1900, and inhabited in 1910 by attorney and Boulder native Henry O. Andrew. In 1929, however, it was transformed into a Mediterranean-style residence by altering the roofline, replacing the porch, stuccoing the walls, and adding new windows. Federal agencies provided employment by

sponsoring modernization projects such as this in local communities during the Depression.

Charles F. Hauck purchased the residence, and Glen Huntington supervised the revision. As an architect, Huntington gave Boulder a significant amount of its present historic flavor and was involved in the design of many houses on 12th and 13th Streets.

Hauck was president and manager of the Hygienic Ice and Coal Company. He also operated the Hygienic Swimming Pool next door, using warm water produced from manufacturing the ice. Renamed Spruce Pool, it continues to welcome swimmers at 21st and Pearl Streets.

Jennifer and Bob Haney discovered this University Hill home for sale in 1990. Their growing family had sought a community amenable to kids and made the transfer here from California. Jennifer, a former creator of Fresh Produce apparel, frankly says, "At the time, it was a big scary house, empty for two years, and screaming to get help. As we surveyed the basement, a sleeping bag there started moving."

The kitchen was decoupaged with magazine recipe pages; elsewhere, walls were dark brown. Haney was in her bold color phase, so she changed to interior colors like glowing cantaloupe and pale chartreuse. As she remarks, "I want to be in a space where I feel alive."

She prefers vintage houses and once reclaimed a Longmont farmhouse being readied for moving. "It is the rural retreat we wanted," she says. "These houses have obviously been good to generations, and we benefit from that."

TRICK DOG

Mango House

(As told by Mark Riley)

From Boston, we surveyed Colorado and California for that place where life would slow down. Candice and I wanted a real town, not a resort, and we'd looked for a community that was interested in education. She's now a Boulder schoolteacher.

We discovered this house painted in its present colors. The turquoise trim had been there forever; the owners from whom we bought added the mango, and on the side porch they really let their artistic side have sway. It incorporates the colors lime, periwinkle, and fuchsia. We wouldn't have risked such colors, but the owners knew what they were doing; for us, it needed no modification.

We took ownership in 2005, after updating baths and kitchen, restaining and repainting. The bones of the house are intact. We didn't want a modern great room; the separate functional spaces worked well for us.

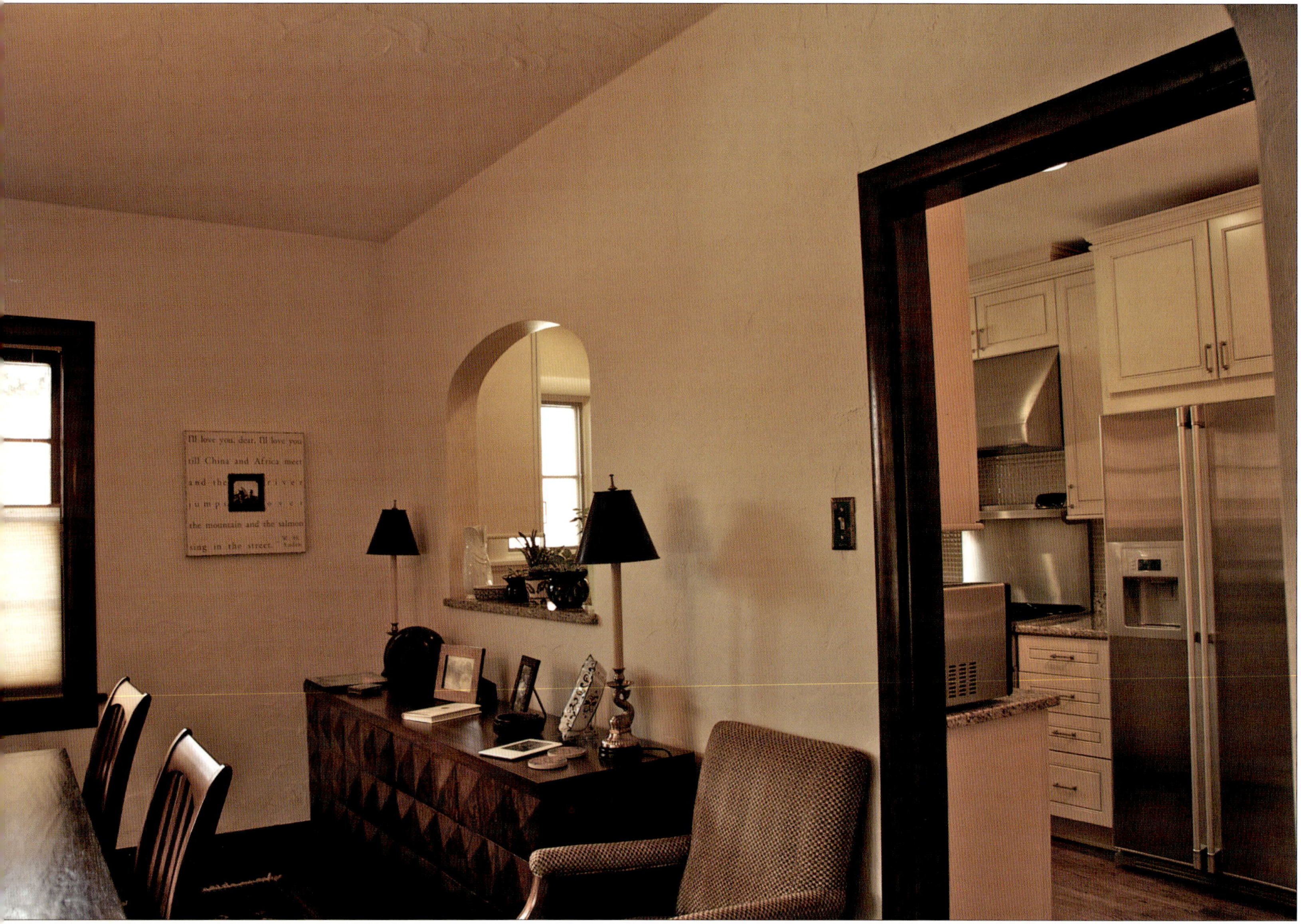
I'll love you, dear, I'll love you
till China and Africa meet
the mountain and the salmon
sing in the street.

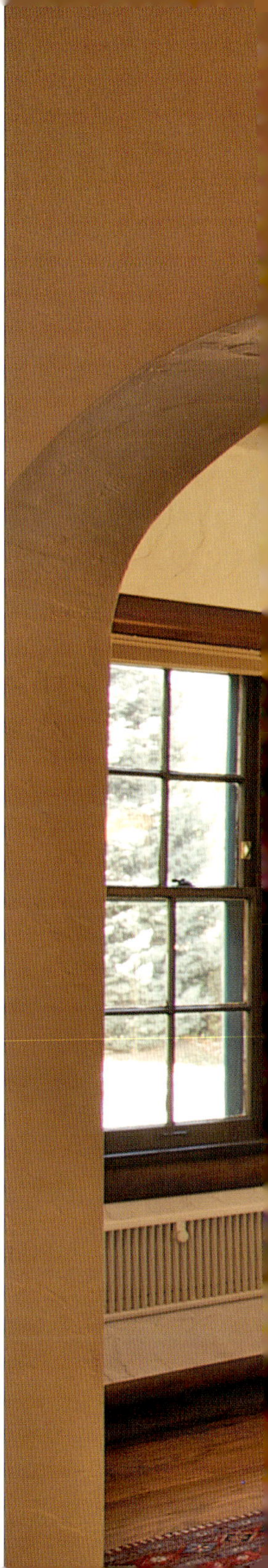

What we love here is the interior window frames; they would require a new die tool if made today. We enjoy the coziness of the bungalow character. The barrel ceiling in the living room and the arched entryways are also appealing.

The interior walls are lath and plaster, what was used until the 1950s before drywall was invented; strips made of wood or rock were attached to the wall studs; texturing with plaster requires shaping when wet, then sanding. This craft is hard to find today.

Emotion often prompts our art collection. We were married in Bali and purchased two canvases done by apparently well-known Balinese artists. Some may

think our way of collecting is too sentimental, but this is a home, not an art gallery.

Our neighborhood is known as University Place. Here, in 1929, Glenn Huntington created our house with its Santa Barbara design. He was Boulder's first full-time resident architect. His work in Boulder includes several houses built in various revival styles, at least five sororities, the Boulder County Courthouse, Boulder High School, and the Band Shell.

Margaret Read, the first woman architect in Boulder and a Huntington associate, designed the classic Santa Barbara–style home next door in 1928. A close look reveals swirling, curving trim and edges.

755

Warming Up to a '20s Energy Home

Back in 1980, Lisa Magee called her husband. She'd found their home. She told him it was kind of Mediterranean. Glenn arrived to see the courtyard of recycled bricks and the path to the front door made of rough-hewn tree stumps. The house was dark and cold with red velvet curtains and glass door panels made of wine bottle bottoms. Glenn, though, had only to see the marvelous view of the Flatirons and the rock wall creating his own oasis, to be sold.

The Magees learned that this was one of two historic Public Service show homes. The formerly innovative twin structures were next-door neighbors and had been built by Boulder's Public Service Company in 1929. Originally, they each featured a "state-of-the-art" coal-fired boiler. Eight-inch-thick terra-cotta-tile building blocks yielded stout, well-insulated walls. The three-way switches could operate the same light from more than one location. The home also featured bow-tie downspouts.

When the roof started leaking, and patching was no longer an option, Glenn wanted to maintain its unique character. He meticulously mapped out the placement and color of each roof tile. Then he contacted building sites and tile manufacturers throughout the state to pick up a dozen tiles here and there. A year later, the rooftop puzzle had a solution.

While the home's layout is far from Lisa's ideal, with lots of small randomly placed rooms, it has served the family well through the years, providing for three kids growing up, moving out, and back in again, as well as a last haven for Lisa's mom.

Today the backyard is even more of an oasis, with ponds, waterfalls, and numerous gardens. Like the interior, it has grown to reflect the needs of the family and shows how eclectic tastes and lots of pets and family can fit happily into a small space, both inside and out.

Grant Place is a four-block, one-way street, beginning at the entrance to Chautauqua Park and dead-ending down at Columbia Cemetery. Even before the Magees became a part of it in 1980, there was the tradition of the Grant Place block party. The street is closed off once a year for this event.

This house has been the family's only home, and the neighborhood an extended family. They can't imagine living anywhere else.

The other historic Public Service show home is next door to the Magees.

Coming Home to an Elegant Landmark

(As told by Joe Stepanek)

We've been away forever it seems. My father was with the United Nations in the late 1940s and '50s. So, for a time as a small child, I lived in China—on a dirt floor. We actually had paper windows. We'd lived in Boulder on Lincoln Place, but left for China in 1947. In 1956, I met my wife Caroline here in Boulder when we were students at Casey Junior High. After our marriage, we were back and forth from this town to places such as Bangladesh, Kenya, and Zambia until I retired from my own overseas job with the U.S. Agency for International Development.

Now we live in this wonderfully old and solid Fountain Formation sandstone home. David Hull Holmes, who built the house in 1922, was Caroline's great uncle. He quarried the exterior stone from land he owned next to Red Rocks, just west of Boulder. Caroline visited him here in the 1950s as an awe-struck child, affected by the mansion's beauty and her uncle and aunt's formality.

She had no idea then that her parents, Judge Horace B. and June Holmes, inheritors of the house, would, out-of-the-blue, offer to let the two of us buy it when I retired and we returned to Boulder. We've been keeping the home in the family for thirteen years now.

In Boulder, Holmes designed several houses, and he lived in this one for thirty years, until 1967. He died at the age of ninety-three and is buried in Green Mountain Cemetery. This house became a historic landmark in 1990.

Uncle David chose an Italian Renaissance style for this home, but mixed in his own preferences. The lower level, designed as a gentleman's billiard room, has ceiling beams that extend through the walls to the foundation's exterior [vegas]. The use of adobe architecture likely came out of the period 1899 to 1913, when Uncle David lived and designed in Tucson.

Other innovative features of the 1920s were ceilings curved at their walls and soft lighting installed behind molding. Holmes also concealed the roof's rain gutters, then trimmed the down spouts with a fleur-de-lis design [a stylized lily that is a symbol of France].

Java, Bali, and Safari is how we now refer to three of the rooms here—living spaces that blend the souvenirs from our homes abroad with the Italian antiques that have always been in this house. We never dreamed we'd have enough rooms to unpack everything. It is enriching to know the history at 720 11th Street. Returning to our Boulder family and friends is the most fulfilling of all because many people in our Foreign Service have no home.

Living with Positive Energy

In 1989, Sheila Hearn-Frost traveled to Boulder and saw its only completely octagonal house in the neighborhood of University Hill. The house was on the market; Ms. Hearn-Frost walked in and knew it was her fate to live there.

The conversation with her daughter went like this: "Look at that funky old house!" "Mom, it has a fireplace in the upstairs master bedroom, just what you've always wanted."

Ms. Hearn-Frost returned to California, where she was a stockbroker, and the next day she told her boss, "I'm eligible for early retirement and I'm moving to Boulder."

Growing up on the East Coast, she had seen and admired this style of home. Close to two hundred of them remain in New York, whereas less than five exist in Colorado. In all, a few hundred survived after their introduction in 1849 by amateur architect Orson Squire Fowler.

The main thing about the octagon style is that it is formed so as to take maximum advantage of the sun's heat and light. Parts of such a house are naturally bright and warm all day.

Boulder's octagon dwelling was built by brick mason Benjamin Franklin Gregg in 1907. For decades, it stood alone on Lincoln Place. Unusual for this building design, there are large windows, such as the semicircular one on the façade, and there is an upstairs skylight.

"There's only one room in the house that has four walls," Ms. Hearn-Frost comments, indicating the dining room where another fireplace is surrounded by geometric brickwork. The bungalow-style flooring here and in the living room is laid in a pattern that aims at a square in the very center of the room.

The owner says, "The woman from whom I obtained my home would remodel and then sell houses. She had the idea to paint the front door rose." She also banished the orange shag carpeting and pea green walls. During upstairs construction, some of the original wood from the house ended up at the dump; it was this devoted decorator who learned what had happened, then retrieved and restored it.

Ms. Hearn-Frost's son-in-law, a cabinetmaker, constructed a window seat in the entryway and a built-in dining room china cabinet that matches the connecting French doors. One of his associates found antique door molding that matched the pieces remaining in the house. He purchased it at a Denver warehouse—which burned down the next day!

The many display areas host collections of complementary-colored objects, paperweights, and dolls, including a wooden penny doll carved during the Revolutionary War era. "In 1775, she cost a penny," says the owner.

About her home, she adds, "I like to think that its geometric shape is conducive to and attracts positive energy."

Prochainement
Tournée du
Chat
Noir
de
Rodolphe Salis
PORTO

1510

An Early Boulder Commune

(As told by Larry Kaptein)

We learned the history of Floral Park when we bought this house in 1992. It was built in 1939, when eight professors at CU needed homes and needed them low-priced. They knew there was a piece of land for sale near Chautauqua for the price of the back taxes owed on it. They were also aware that some useful building materials had been sent to the dump after a school in Boulder had been torn down.

With the bricks from the demolished school and the inexpensive land purchase, they created a housing development with Glen Huntington, Boulder's first full-time resident architect. All eight houses feature bricks painted white and red roof tiles; they share a garage structure and a green space.

I've often wondered whether this neighborhood might be part of the genesis for Boulder's philosophical point of view. In Floral Park we meet twice a year to socialize and discuss property management issues. It's a historic district, so the neighborhood maintains the look of its Monterey Colonial style.

Fortunately, there's also the opportunity to individualize and remodel. I know nothing of gardening, but two marble posts I found on our property inspired me to landscape our backyard.

I located the posts at the opening from the back of our property to the Commons, the shared Floral Park green space. The Asian appearance of the posts presented me with a garden design theme. I'd placed some sculpture here and there, and wanted to add to the collection.

I discovered Mile High Statuary, located in Denver, south of Casa Bonita. It's a vast parking lot with rows and rows of cherubs and fountains. Inside it's like a wild sorcerer's workplace. I was given a book containing every imaginable sculptural theme. I chose the colors I desired. They'll use molds to create my selections, and then I'm looking forward to decorating with them.

Flagstaff Road

Flagstaff Towers

(As told by Linda Jourgensen)

In 1970, there was a common style of house that looked to me like a mineshaft. We read about and contacted architect Chuck Haertling, believing he would not suggest the mineshaft style. We'd recently arrived in Boulder, and wanted a new house. We had heard that mould accumulated in older homes, and our oldest child had asthma.

We wanted to live right in the area, so we purchased an 11,000-square-foot piece of property just up Flagstaff Road. The only thing was, most of our land went downhill. That dictated our design. Instead of a sprawling house, we needed one that was vertical. We made simple drawings ourselves, but never envisioned the towers Chuck devised.

The towers became the framework—four of them. There, Haertling stowed the most practical aspects of a dwelling: bathrooms, closets, and heating system (including a sauna). The other rooms were cantilevered [seeming to project in space without support] from the towers and supported by heavy rebar.

There are four stories: bedrooms, then kitchen and living room, master suite, then office space on top. We have several views of the panorama of central Boulder. The core of the house is a circular staircase supported by an iron fire pole. My daughter learned to go between a surrounding network of bars and down the fire pole; she did so without fanfare one day, landing in the kitchen. The mountain was a playground for the kids and that's one of the things we loved about it.

Haertling installed some very plain and natural elements. The towers are made of painted concrete blocks. The rest of the house is covered with copper strips seamed together by hand. The entryway has an aggregate floor containing a mixture of pebbles that our grandson struggled to crawl on as a baby.

The house feels utilitarian. Wall lighting is essentially two light bulbs placed together vertically, one up and one down.

Partial to built-ins, Haertling installed a concrete kitchen table that was a disaster, really. It was way too high for normal chairs. It was a simple triangle that jutted out from the wall, so at least we could easily clean the floor underneath. One day we simply couldn't go on living with it, and chopped it to pieces.

Like a Clamshell

(As told by Diana Kahn)

Almost a tree house, our home is characterized first by all the glass through which we see Boulder from Flagstaff Road. You can't hang pictures on glass. The view is the pictures. In the late '60s we wanted a place with minimal landscape upkeep, and we liked contemporary design. In this location, natural landscaping makes sense. At the time in Boulder, architect Charles Haertling was the only one in town doing experimental things.

When completed in 1969, our home's main floor was like a thick sandwich of glass. At the corners, glass edges abut each other a la Frank Lloyd Wright. We eventually wanted additional warmth in the house. Had we altered the glass design, new city rules would have required our reducing the amount of glass.

To preserve our original walls, we used a film applied by Sun-Ease Window Tinting. The product has helped us maintain a more comfortable indoor temperature year-round.

Another issue with the original design was that it created huge icicles on the house. The roof appears to be concrete, but is actually plywood covered with rubber sheeting. The solution Haertling used was walnut chips that gave texture to a special paint. The texture keeps the snow melting slower—no more four-foot icicles.

Our house represents a clamshell, part of Haertling's organic style, emphasizing harmony between human habitation and the natural world. The architect's Leaneagh house, with its roof shaped like an aspen leaf, is a similar example in Boulder. The Jorgensen house, built simultaneously next door, has vertical lines and shapes that illustrate another style Haertling employed: mathematical and geometric themes.

He was protective of the esthetics of his architecture. That's why he insisted, against our preferences, that the bathrooms be windowless. Windows would have destroyed the exterior look he wanted.

This living room is forty feet off the ground. Forty-foot pilings were driven into the hill to support the house. That was the biggest construction expense.

There were complaints that our house ruined the mountainside, was too contemporary for the Boulder look, and stood out in the morning sun. We never wanted to put it on historic tours. Once, though, we were asked to bring in a group of September School students to view a Haertling creation.

A boy of sixteen on the tour saw our gate, designed by weaver Helen Wilson and constructed by the then Walker Welding Company. He said, "My dad built that gate when he was my age."

North Boulder

Keeping It in the Family

(As told by Judy Dayhoff)

In 1881, my great granddad, Swiss immigrant Wendolin Moll, homesteaded 160 acres north of Boulder near Left Hand Canyon. [The Homestead Act was a law passed in the 1860s that offered up to 160 acres of public land to any head of a family who paid a registration fee, lived on the land for five years, and cultivated it or built on it.] I grew up on 80 acres of the same property, in my parents' house.

Starting in 1967, and for the following twenty years, my husband Ronnie built a shop, a shed, and our house on some of this same land. Our dads helped out. During that time we lived in a mobile

home on the property. We hauled all the moss rock on the house's exterior and interior from hills on this land in an old yellow jeep; Ronnie's Uncle Hubert did the stonework.

My dad had a herd of Holsteins and a dairy farm here in the 1950s. Now, the neighbor's cattle graze part of the property in the summertime.

Irrigation water has been available via the Haldi Ditch using Left Hand Ditch Company water. The company was formed in the nineteenth century and continues to operate much as it did then. Landowners within the company's territory purchase shares of water. A ditch rider releases sufficient water to cover the orders early each morning.

As a child, I saved to buy a horse. My lifelong friend Alice and I would ride down country roads and on her folks' ranch. I continued to keep horses until ten years ago. Alice and I would share the feeding chores for the animals. If snow prevented us from driving into Alice's ranch, we sometimes walked a couple of miles round trip.

Ronnie and I prefer the Victorian style, but we built our home using plans that we thought suited the landscape. Our furnishings are nostalgic pieces, many passed down through both sides of the family. After our marriage, we were away for a few years when Ronnie had an assignment in New Mexico. It was, and is, so nice to come back to the Gould Family Farm.

North Boulder landscape